Old HELENSBURGH, RHU & SHA

by
John Hood

Despite first impressions, this elaborate piece of machinery appears to be nothing more complicated than an early lawnmower! Posing with it are the gardeners of Camis Eskan House, one of Helensburgh's larger residences, which was the home of the Dennistouns of Colgrain until its conversion in the 1930s to a tuberculosis sanatorium. From the 1950s it was a geriatric hospital but this closed in 1977 and patients were transferred to Vale of Leven Hospital. It was converted into luxury apartments in 1979.

First published in the United Kingdom, 1999,
by Stenlake Publishing, Ochiltree Sawmill, The Lade,
Ochiltree, Ayrshire, KA18 2NX
Telephone / Fax: 01290 423114

ISBN 1 84033 065 1

THE PUBLISHERS REGRET THAT THEY CANNOT SUPPLY
COPIES OF ANY PICTURES FEATURED IN THIS BOOK.

ACKNOWLEDGEMENTS

The publishers wish to thank Robert Grieves for permission to reproduce
the pictures on pages 10, 16, 32 and the inside back cover, and Dave Crocker
who provided the rest of the pictures in the book from his collection. The
author also wishes to acknowledge the assistance given to him by the staff
of Helensburgh Library.

In addition to the attractions of floral decorations, illuminations and a
multitude of tearooms and ice cream kiosks, summer shows were also
staged in Helensburgh to entertain the holidaymaker. For example, patrons
of the 1927 Summer Concert Party Season, held at Breingan's bandstand,
could feast their eyes on performances by the girls of Slick Ltd – 'a specially
selected company of talented artistes direct from Opera House, Perth'!
Accompanying the girls were the Troon Entertainers, the Cheerio
Entertainers, a popular Glasgow concert party, and the celebrated Imperial
Scots, who were appearing prior to their English tour.

INTRODUCTION

The Burgh of Helensburgh lies within the former Parish of Rhu (or Row, as it was known until 1927) which was formed in 1648. The parish stretched some fourteen miles along the eastern shore of the Gare Loch and its earliest community was formed around a church and a ferry at the rudha (or point).

By the eighteenth century the parish was renowned for its herring and salmon fishing and a hundred local boats operated on the loch. The area was also purported to be the haunt of smugglers and even rated a mention in Scott's *Heart of Midlothian*. Indeed, when George IV visited the Duke of Argyll at Rosneath Castle in the 1830s, he is supposed to have expressed a wish to sample some illicit whisky and was taken by ferry to Rhu where a barrel was duly procured.

In the 1750s the lands of Malig, or Millig, to the south of the parish were purchased by Sir James Colquhoun of Luss who intended creating a community of 'bonnet-makers, stocking, linen and woollen weavers'. In 1776 he placed an advertisement in *The Glasgow Journal* offering land for sale and his initiative led to the creation of New Town, which he later called Helensburgh in honour of his wife. In 1777 the plan for the town was drawn up by the surveyor Charles Ross in a grid pattern of long wide streets running east to west, intersected at intervals by shorter streets running north to east. This pattern was maintained by the Glasgow surveyor Peter Fleming in a later extension in 1803.

Between 1802, when it was granted burgh status, and 1897, when the Municipal Buildings were erected, the town steadily expanded. In 1846 a gas supply was introduced and in 1868 the water supply was improved with the opening of the Mains Hill Reservoir. Furthermore, in 1862 Helensburgh became a *quoad sacra* parish and a cemetery was opened locally to relieve the congestion in Rhu churchyard which had been the only cemetery in the parish.

Throughout the nineteenth century, the district's outstanding scenery and clean air encouraged many wealthy Glasgow merchants to build handsome villas along the seafront or on higher ground overlooking the River Clyde and the Gare Loch. Due to a lack of decent roads, communication had traditionally been by boat and the original plan for Helensburgh included a harbour, although this and the subsequent pier were never totally successful. It was not until Bell's *Comet* revolutionised river travel, bringing regular sailings to and from Glasgow, that the town began to develop as a resort for the tourists from the city. In 1857 development of Helensburgh was further enhanced when the Glasgow, Dumbarton & Helensburgh Railway Company extended their line to link the town with Glasgow.

In the first half of the twentieth century, Helensburgh benefited from new facilities and attractions such as Hermitage Park, the outdoor bathing pool, two cinemas and, in the 1920s and '30s, new housing. From the 1950s onwards, however, piers were closed – firstly at Helensburgh, then on Gare Loch, followed in the early 1970s by Craigendoran – and steamer services ceased. But despite this the town continues to attract many visitors and as it approaches the new millennium it can certainly reflect with satisfaction on its history.

Contrary to Sir James Colquhoun's original plan to develop Helensburgh as a model industrial town, it was as a seaside resort that the burgh flourished. Known as the 'Brighton of Scotland' and 'Garden Town of the Firth of Clyde', holidaymakers would flock to the town by steamer and train for a trip to the seaside and gradually the seafront was taken up by long esplanades, gift shops and restaurants to cater for the many visitors.

In 1877, due to fierce opposition from Helensburgh residents who didn't approve of a railway station being built on the seafront, the North British Railway Company abandoned its plans to build a terminal alongside the town's pier in favour of a new station and pier at Craigendoran. The station was officially opened in May 1882 and for generations of holidaymakers who travelled on the North British (or 'NB') boats, it was the gateway to destinations such as Rothesay and Dunoon. From August 1894, those wishing to travel to the north of Scotland were also catered for as the station became the starting point of the West Highland line to Fort William.

THE PIER, CRAIGENDORAN

The North British Steam Packet Company, a subsidiary of the North British Railway, ran daily steamer services out of Craigendoran in direct competition with other railway companies such as the Caledonian and the Glasgow & South Western (who operated out of Wemyss Bay and Gourock respectively). From the 1930s, until closure in 1972, the pier's fortunes steadily declined; but many will remember the NB boats, all bearing names associated with the works of Sir Walter Scott, such as *Meg Merrilees*, *Lucy Ashton* and *Waverley*, and easily recognised by their distinctive red funnels with white bands and black tops.

Waverley at Craigendoran

C34

This postcard of passengers disembarking from the *Waverley* at Craigendoran Pier in the 1920s gives some idea of the popularity of trips 'doon the watter'. Not to be confused with the present-day paddle steamer of the same name, this vessel entered service in the 1920s as a replacement for the *Redgauntlet* but was requisitioned as a minesweeper during the Second World War and sunk at Dunkirk while rescuing troops from the beaches. The present *Waverley*, which entered service in 1947 as a replacement for the 61 year old *Lucy Ashton*, was the last steamer to be based at Craigendoran. It was withdrawn from service in 1973 and sold to the Paddle Steamer Preservation Society for the grand sum of one penny!

Stretching from Queen's Hotel to the Old Parish Church, the area along the seafront at East Bay represented an expansion of Helensburgh as, until 1835, its boundaries had extended from the Millig Burn on the east to the Glenan Burn on the west. Although there have been some changes to East Clyde Street, many of the properties seen here have survived. The skyline too is virtually unchanged, with the exception of the Maitland Street gasometer, which is now to the left of the square tower of St Columba's Church.

EAST BAY, HELENSBURGH.

The East and West Bay esplanades were laid out in the 1880s, financed by a combination of public subscription and a donation from Sir James Colquhoun (a descendant of the town's founder). They provided Helensburgh with an almost unbroken promenade walk from East Bay to Kidston Park, made all the more pleasant by grassy areas, ample seating and, of course, the obligatory tearoom! Almost all the buildings behind the tearoom (which is now the premises of Helensburgh Auto Spares) have survived, albeit with some minor alterations. Just above the trees can be seen the little cupolas of Clyde Street School, which was opened in 1903 by the Parish Council of Row as a replacement for the Grant Street Industrial (or 'Ragged') School.

EAST CLYDE STREET LOOKING EAST, HELENSBURGH.

E02530

East Clyde Street, pictured from the foot of Sinclair Street in 1913. While the tall tenement building to the left has survived, some of the properties beyond this have been replaced by a modern car dealership. On the opposite side of the street, to the far right, is the gable wall of the Old Parish Church, the site of which is now occupied by a complex of flats known as Tower Court. The buildings further east have survived, as has the former Clyde Street School, which is hidden among the trees.

McFarlane's Gareloch Motor Service Co. Ltd was probably the earliest motor bus company in Dunbartonshire and actually pre-dated the introduction of the tramcars. Services from Helensburgh were operated to Dumbarton, Garelochhead and Clynder, along with tours to Aberfoyle and the Trossachs. Here the bus fleet, including Wolseley and Albion buses, is pictured outside the company premises at the granary building in West Clyde Street, c. 1906.

WEST CLYDE STREET FROM SINCLAIR STREET, HELENSBURGH.   E02524

Another 1913 view of Clyde Street from the foot of Sinclair Street, but this time looking west. The wine merchants to the right of picture (coincidentally, now Oddbins) was formerly the Clachan public house. This was referred to by local businessmen as 'The Presbytery', possibly because of its close proximity to the Old Parish Church, but also, it is said, to 'dignify' their visits to the pub! To the left is the frontage of the granary, which was considered an eyesore by the locals. It was demolished in 1980, having been a malt barn, a bus depot, a garage and, from 1934, a restaurant.

The venue for the 2nd Annual Sandcastle Competition held in August 1915 was the beach east of Sinclair Street. The competition, inaugurated by Councillor Morrison, was mounted for all children, resident or visitor. On this occasion, the Parks Department had begun preparations for the competition as early as 6 a.m. when the area was roped off and each 'claim' pegged out. Despite anxiety over the weather, the sun shone and a great day was enjoyed by all!

Some 220 competitors (an increase of 130 from the previous year) took part in the competition. In contrast to the first one, which placed no restrictions on adornments, only materials found on the beach were permitted to be used on this occasion. Inevitably, the lack of flags and such meant that the displays were less colourful, but nonetheless numerous forts, battleships and dug-outs (reflecting the obvious spirit of patriotism) were constructed in order to impress the judge, a Mrs. J.F.P. Duncan. Indeed, little Joe Handyside scooped 1st Prize with his bugle sculptured in the sand, accompanied by the message: 'Fall in'!

Sinclair Street (previously known as the Old Luss Road) has always been one of Helensburgh's principal thoroughfares and perfectly illustrates the intentions of its founder, Sir James Colquhoun, to develop a planned layout of broad intersecting streets. Many of the properties in this view from the 1930s still stand, most notably St Columba's Church with its distinctive square tower and, opposite, the more ornate Municipal Buildings on the corner of East Princes Street. The building to the left (now the premises of John Menzies) still has its cast iron decoration along the bottom of the roof. The tall sandstone building on the right once housed the premises of W.G. Christie, a well-known grocer and provision merchant who established his business in 1861.

This 1904 postcard of the interior of W.G. Christie's shop on Sinclair Street appears to have been a corporate Christmas card and advertisement rolled into one! While 'Compliments of the Season' are printed on the reverse, there are also adverts for: 'Cheese – 1 ton prize dairy cheddars from Kilmarnock, October Show, 1904; Specialty [*sic*] – a few finest old cheddars, Champion Dairy, October Show, 1903; Dunlops – usual fine Dairy of Dunlop cheese for toasting'

A 'motorman's holiday' preparing to depart from the premises of Waldie & Co. on Sinclair Street. As well as hiring coaches, the firm was also a motor bus operator and funeral undertaker.

Dominating the corner of Sinclair Street and East Princes Street are the rather ornate Municipal Buildings, erected in 1878 to a design by Glasgow architect John Honeyman. This building replaced the earlier Town Hall (itself a conversion of the town's first theatre) which stood on the same spot. The 1906 extension on Sinclair Street, designed by local architect, A.N. Paterson, was built to house the fire station and police office. At the main entrance to the latter can still be seen an engraved set of handcuffs on either side of the doorway. A discerning eye will also notice the stone effigy of a cat to the right of the police office entrance. This is said to have been added by Paterson in fondness for a feline who frequented the site during building works.

1 August 1908 was a day of celebration in Helensburgh in honour of twenty year old Private George Gray of the 5th Scottish Rifles. A local lad, Private Gray had won the King's Prize for marksmanship in a competition where he was up against selected marksmen from throughout the British Empire. In honour of the occasion, banners and flags decorated Princes Street, Sinclair Street, the Municipal Buildings and the Railway Station (which was closed to the public for the day). A reception was held in the Council Chambers for the young soldier and afterwards, accompanied by Provost Bryden, he headed a procession through the town.

WEST CLYDE STREET LOOKING EAST, HELENSBURGH.

E 02522

In the early 1900s West Clyde Street featured Breingan's bandstand (erected in 1902 in memory of ex-Provost Breingan), the granary and the Old Parish Church. Before the church was built in 1847, the granary had been used for worship. All have now been demolished and only the Italian style clock tower survives, this having been converted into a tourist information centre.

The foresight of the town councillors in creating a broad esplanade is justified by the bustle in this photograph from 1935. Many of the buildings remain today, including the Woolworth store and the Imperial Hotel. The hotel was a popular staging post for coaches heading towards the steamers at Balloch and Loch Lomond. The pier head arch and booking office is to the right of the Granary Restaurant.

The Duchess Of Argyll, Princess Louise, who lived at Rosneath Castle, arriving at Helensburgh Pier to attend the presentation of new Troop Flags to the Rosneath & Kilcreggan Boy Scouts of which she was patron. Although bunting was strung up and the crowds came out in full force, the pier's facilities were somewhat limited and it is obvious that no attempt could be made to protect the Princess from the bleak winter weather!

Despite its rather grand appearance, Helensburgh pier was never as successful as Craigendoran's, not least because the shallowness of the river at this point made steamer operations difficult. Initially, in 1816, a rough stone dyke had been constructed on the site of the present pier for use as a landing stage and, as late as 1834, a horse-drawn wagon was used to take passengers ashore. While the pier arch was erected in 1898 and the outdoor bathing pool gifted by Bailie Andrew Buchanan in 1928, the facilities were still second best to those at Craigendoran. Whereas rail passengers, prior to boarding the steamers at Craigendoran, disembarked on to the pier itself (which was covered), those using Helensburgh Pier were faced with a brisk ten minute walk from the railway station in East Princes Street to the pier head, before being obliged to walk the length of the pier which was exposed to the elements.

Although any doubts as to the wisdom of erecting outdoor bathing pools in the west of Scotland could be dispelled by this busy scene from the 1930s, in reality only the most hardy would use these pools in all weathers! The site of the pool was infilled and landscaped and a modern indoor pool opened alongside in 1977.

At the turn of the century Helensburgh boasted five art needlework repositories: Stewart at 6 Princes Street, Marchbank at 50 Princes Street, MacNee at 17 Sinclair Street, Dickson at 87 Clyde Street and Mitchell at 31 Clyde Street. Their wares were not restricted to needlework alone and an advertisement from the early 1900s shows that Mrs MacNee also stocked baby linen and ladies underclothing (she was an agent for Madam Worth's corsets!). From the row of books on the table at the left, it appears that this 1914 photograph was taken at a prizegiving.

John Halsey's shop at 32 East Princes Street, opposite the Railway Station, specialised in corned beef and pickled tongues, and was one of several butcher shops in the town. Although only two of the staff are posing for the camera, this 1906 postcard (sent to an Uncle George Halsey in England) explains on the reverse that there were at least another two employees, but 'Johnnie had just gone for his dinner and the other man was up the loch'.

A stormy scene at the pier head which somewhat belies the fact that the Gare Loch is considered a safe anchorage for small craft! It also illustrates the problems faced during the Second World War, when trenches dug on the esplanade as air raid shelters proved unsuitable due to constant flooding. Silhouetted against the murky sky is the Henry Bell monument which was erected in 1872.

LA SCALA, THE POPULAR COSY CINEMA, HELENSBURGH.

Moving pictures were first shown in Helensburgh in 1911 at the Mission Hall in East King Street and the town's first purpose-built cinema, the Picture Palace, was opened in John Street that same year. On Christmas Eve 1913 a second cinema, the La Scala, was opened in James Street and was equipped with the latest technology, including 'tip-up' seats! The Palace, later renamed the Cine House, was eventually closed and replaced in 1927 by the more modern Tower Cinema in Colquhoun Street. In the early 1980s the La Scala was converted to a cinema-cum-snooker hall although the cinema section was closed in 1984.

It is hard to imagine that the broad sweep of Colquhoun Square was once the site of a sandstone quarry which was prone to flooding! This turn of the century view has hardly changed except for the repositioning of the Mercat Cross to the north side of the Square. Made from pink granite, it was gifted to the town in 1903 by Sir James Colquhoun to mark the centenary of the burgh. The story goes that one night, while taking an important local resident past the Cross, a driver misjudged his manoeuvre and almost overturned his coach, whereupon the passenger demanded that the Cross be moved on the grounds of safety.

In 1915 local people turned out in force to pay their respects at the funeral of Provost Bonner's son, who was a victim of Britain's worst rail disaster. On the morning of Saturday, 22 May 1915, a troop train with almost 500 officers and men of the 7th Battalion of the Royal Scots collided with a coal train at Quintinshill, outside Gretna. Minutes later a London to Glasgow express train ploughed into the wreckage, causing further casualties. The vast majority of fatalities were young soldiers, many of whom were trapped among the burning wreckage. In total 227 died (of whom 214 were soldiers) and a further 264 were injured.

A parade in Colquhoun Square of various organisations, including the Boy Scouts complete with wooden staves. The properties east of Colquhoun Street have survived but those to the right, on Princes Street, have mostly been replaced by modern shops and flats.

The Boys' Brigade movement was started in Glasgow in 1883 and before long every town had its local company. By 1927 Helensburgh had two companies, the 1st, attached to the West Free Kirk, and the 2nd, attached to St Columba's Church. Today, both companies are in the process of amalgamating into the 1/2 Helensburgh Boys' Brigade. This is the full company of the 1st Helensburgh outside their hall.

An Arrol Johnston taxi on East Princes Street, *c.* 1906. This view to the east of Princes Street illustrates the systematic way in which Helensburgh was laid out, for it was one of several wide streets running east to west and the original plan specified a street width of sixty feet.

The opening of a station by the Glasgow, Dumbarton & Helensburgh Railway in 1857 was a boost for Helensburgh as it brought the town within easy commuting distance of Glasgow for residents and visitors alike. Originally terminating at George Street, the line was extended to East Princes Street in 1863 and the existing building pictured here (now Helensburgh Central) was opened in 1899. The exterior of the building remains largely unchanged today, as do the tenement properties opposite, which include the former Railway Temperance Hotel.

Station Helensburgh

Today, Helensburgh boasts two stations: the main station pictured here (now Helensburgh Central) and Helensburgh Upper. The latter, at the junction of Sinclair Street and Rossdhu Drive, was opened in 1894 and is on the West Highland line which runs from Craigendoran to Fort William. Helensburgh Central (which is on the central belt network) is very typical of late Victorian railway architecture and the semi-circular glass frontage of the gable end and much of the elaborate cast-iron structure still remains today, although the platform canopy has now been stripped of its glass.

King Street—looking East—Helensburgh.

King Street, east of Sinclair Street, has been extensively altered over the years. While many of the properties on the north side remain (including the Baptist Church, Park Church and St Joseph's Roman Catholic Church), some of the older housing has been replaced by modern flats. Further along King Street is East End Park which was gifted by Sir James Colquhoun to serve as a recreation area for the east end of the town. On the south side of King Street, the medical centre and Somerfield supermarket now occupy the site of the railway coal yard. The gasometer on the right belonged to the Helensburgh Gas Light Company (gas was introduced to the town in 1845). Later, when the gas works were expanded they occupied the site of the Grant Street School which, with the opening of the Clyde Street School, had become surplus to the town's educational requirements.

In the early days of the burgh, people with infectious diseases were treated in a disused malt barn in Maitland Street. By all accounts accommodation was limited and the facilities were rudimentary. A more permanent solution was found in 1875 when the Fever Hospital was built in East King Street, funded by public subscription and a generous bequest from Miss Anne Alexander, a Helensburgh resident. Built with a separate tuberculosis sanatorium, it was said to be 'unsurpassed by any provincial hospital', although it was pointed out that the close proximity of the local cemetery was perhaps 'unfortunate'!

Bowling Greens and Tennis Courts. Helensburgh

C31

Hermitage Park was originally known as Cramb Park because it was laid out around Hermitage House, the home of the Cramb family. It was opened in 1911 after the house and grounds were bought by the town council. During the First World War the house was used as a military auxiliary hospital and between 1918 and 1926 it served as an annexe to Hermitage School, until a new primary school was built nearby. The house then became a town council store before demolition in 1963.

The 'commodious and elegant' building (or 'tin hut', as it was affectionately known) behind the 1st hole is the original clubhouse of Helensburgh Golf Club which was established in 1893. The course was laid out in fields of Kirkmichael Farm and advice on its design was given by golfing legends such as 'Old' Tom Morris of St Andrews and James Braid. Originally a nine hole course, it was extended to eighteen holes in 1905. A notable early committee member was Andrew Bonar Law. In 1900 the clubhouse was relocated closer to Helensburgh Upper Station, presumably for the convenience of members. In 1909 the existing clubhouse was opened by the Duke of Argyll, although having been altered and extended several times over the years, it would be virtually unrecognisable to members from that time.

Helensburgh's curling club was established in 1847. One of the town's first curling ponds was located in East King Street, but in 1896 the pond pictured here was opened in Havelock Street and was capable of accommodating twelve rinks. Later still, a pond was opened on Luss Road, opposite the town's reservoir.

Gifted to the town by William Kidston, Kidston Park is situated halfway between Helensburgh and Rhu on Cairndhu Point, which was once known as Neddy's Point after a fisherman-cum-ferryman who stayed there. The park was opened in 1877 and at one time it had a jetty at the water's edge for the training ship *Empress*. There is now a children's play area and car park, and all that is left of the original bandstand is the concrete base.

Ardencaple Quadrant, Helensburgh.

The original sixty houses in Ardencaple Quadrant were built by the council in the 1920s to provide easily affordable accommodation for local men returning from the First World War. The field and greenhouse to the right once formed part of Ferniegair Estate, which was the family home of William Kidston, a Glasgow merchant and twice Provost of Helensburgh. During his second term of office, Kidston was one of the most vocal opponents to the North British Railway Company extending its line along the sea front to the pier. Ferniegair House has since been replaced by more housing.

The first landing place on the Gare Loch was a stone pier erected in the vicinity of Row Point in 1835 and, at one time, it was the starting place for families heading for the New World. The present-day pier at Rhu was built further east at the foot of Pier Road and was at one time one of eight on the Gare Loch. Later, the bay provided safe mooring for the large yachts belonging to the Glasgow merchants and shipping barons. A coastguard station was opened in 1965 and in 1977, after a period of disuse, the Clyde Port Authority modernised the pier and also built a marina.

This early 1900s photograph shows the properties overlooking Rhu Bay, which has long been a safe anchorage for small craft. Out of picture, on the bay further to the east at Spy's Lane, were thatched cottages known as the shore cottages of Laggerie (an old local name), and to the west of the Colquhoun Arms was Ferry Acres, where cattle once grazed. For many years the Colquhoun Arms was a popular staging post on the old Gare Loch road. Even today, coaches run by Wilson of Rhu still leave from this spot at the bottom of Manse Brae.

The Post Office with its distinctive Dutch style roof is unchanged today and the Colquhoun Arms still plies its trade, although it has been renamed the Rhu Inn. Amazingly, there were once as many as thirty hostelries in Rhu parish. In the 1830s this was said to be deplored by a local minister, the Rev. John Laurie, whose opinion was that two would have been 'abundantly sufficient'!

ROW, VILLAGE

Manse Brae has changed little from when this photograph was taken. The property to the extreme left still stands and adjoins the Rhu Inn, although the small cottage has been replaced by the premises of Wilson of Rhu. Beyond the cottage, the newsagent-cum-tearoom is now The Brae Shop, a newsagents and general store, and the wooden structure (which has always been a joinery yard, and is now Spy's the joiners) has remarkably remained the same.

Row was the scene of the infamous Row Heresy Trial of 1831, which saw the minister, John Campbell McLeod, charged with teaching heresy. Despite support from his congregation, the case went to the General Assembly, who found against him and stripped him of his office. The present church, built in 1851, was designed by the local architect, William Spence. Funded by donations from, among others, Sir James Colquhoun and Robert Napier, it was enlarged in 1891 when the north walls were extended forward. Henry Bell and the captain of the *Comet*, Captain Bain, are buried in the churchyard.

At Shandon, situated a few miles up the coast from Rhu, is Garemouth which was one of several large Victorian houses converted for use as holiday or convalescent homes for city children (some with respiratory problems). Renamed the Agnes Millar Wilson Home, it was also used for the 'Glasgow poor children's fresh air fortnight'. This was a scheme partly run by Glasgow Corporation's Education Department to give poor children from the city an annual holiday in the country or at the seaside. This rather glum group of kids featured on a postcard dated 1925. On the reverse the writer tells us 'Our new lot came on Friday. They are nice children, but are uproarious at times. We have 34, but many more come next Friday'.

Shandon was once the exclusive preserve of wealthy merchants who, throughout the nineteenth century, built large houses with outstanding views across the Gare Loch. Initially, residents were reliant on sailing ships and then steamers as their means of communication with the rest of the country, but in 1894 the West Highland railway line was opened and a station was built at Shandon, providing an alternative means of travel. It is said that not all residents welcomed this new development, as they thought it would encroach upon their relative isolation, so they purchased land to the rear of their properties to force the railway company to move the track to higher ground.

Most of the Victorian villas were extremely well-appointed, but of all of them the most outstanding was probably West Shandon, the home of Robert Napier, one of Scotland's top marine engineers. His house was designed by John Thomas Rochhead and included a museum and picture gallery to hold Napier's extensive collection. On Napier's death in 1876 the house was sold and reopened as the Shandon Hydropathic, complete with Russian, Turkish and salt water baths and, obviously, a conservatory! During both world wars the house was requisitioned for used by the Navy, but after the Second World War it became a hotel before being demolished in 1957.